LOOK CLOSER

SWAMP LIFE

PHOTOGRAPHED BY
JANE BURTON & KIM TAYLOR

WRITTEN BY
THERESA GREENAWAY

DORLING KINDERSLEY
LONDON · NEW YORK · STUTTGART

A DORLING KINDERSLEY BOOK

Editor Deborah Murrell **Art editor** Val Wright
Senior editor Christiane Gunzi **Designer** Floyd Sayers
Design assistants Nicola Rawson, Lucy Bennett
Production Louise Barratt
Illustrations Nick Hall
Index Jane Parker
Managing editor Sophie Mitchell
Managing art editor Miranda Kennedy
U.S. editor B. Alison Weir

Consultants
Geoff Boxshall, Theresa Greenaway, Gordon Howes,
Mark O'Shea, Tim Parmenter, Matthew Robertson, Edward Wade

With thanks to Paul Clark and Mark O'Shea for supplying
some of the animals and information in this book.

Endpapers photographed by Peter Scoones, Planet Earth Pictures

First American Edition, 1993
10 9 8 7 6 5 4 3 2 1
Published in the United States by
Dorling Kindersley, Inc., 232 Madison Avenue, New York, New York, 10016

Published in Great Britain by Dorling Kindersley Limited.
Distributed by Houghton Mifflin Company, Boston, Massachusetts.

Library of Congress Cataloging-in-Publication Data
Greenaway, Theresa, 1947-
Swamp life / by Theresa Greenaway ; photography by Kim Taylor and Jane Burton. –1st American ed.
p. cm. – (Look closer)
Includes index.
Summary: Discusses the animals and plants that live in swamps.
Includes caiman, snapping turtles, and water lettuce.
ISBN 1-56458-211-6
1. Swamp fauna–Juvenile literature. 2. Swamp plants–Juvenile literature.
[1. Swamp animals. 2. Swamp plants.] I. Taylor, Kim, ill. II. Burton, Jane, ill. III. Title. IV. Series.
QH87.3.G74 1993
574.5'26325–dc20
92-53489-CIP-AC
Color reproduction by Colourscan, Singapore
Printed and bound in Italy by New Interlitho, Milan

CONTENTS

Look for us, and we will show you the size of every animal and plant that you read about in this book.

LIFE IN A SWAMP

The purple gallinule
(Porphyrio porphyrio)
is 8 in. long.
It lives in Australasia, Europe, India,
Indonesia, North Africa, and the
Middle East.

The red mangrove's
(Rhizophora mangle)
leaves are 6 in. long.
It lives in the Americas.

A SWAMP IS AN AREA of land covered in still or slow-moving water, with plants growing in and around it. All sorts of fascinating animals and plants make their homes in swamps, including snapping turtles and water hyacinths. Only a few kinds of trees can grow in such waterlogged conditions, and these have roots that stick out of the water to take in air. The only trees that can grow in salt water are mangroves. They form a thick jungle along quiet tropical coastlines, where the tide goes in and out twice a day. Among their tangled branches, an amazing array of animals climbs, leaps, and flies. The mangrove swamps are vital to their survival. Mangroves are important to people, too, because their roots prevent the coastline from being washed away by the sea.

The green iguana's
(Iguana iguana)
body is 6 in. long.
It lives in Central and
South America, and
the Caribbean.

**The young
spectacled caiman**
(Caiman crocodilus)
is 18 in. long.
It lives in Central and South
America, and Florida.

The fiddler crab's
(Uca vocans)
shell is 1/2 in. wide.
It lives in Africa, Australia,
India, Indonesia, and
southern Asia.

The archer fish
(Toxotes chatereus)
is 4 in. long.
It lives in Australia, India,
and Southeast Asia.

The mangrove snake's
(*Boiga dendrophila
melanota*)
head is 2 in. long.
It lives in Southeast Asia.

he mudskipper
Periophthalmus barbarus)
4 1/4 in. long.
lives in Australia, East
frica, India, Southeast Asia,
nd the South Pacific Islands.

The spiny-bellied orb weaver's
(*Gasteracantha cancriformis*)
body is 1/2 in. wide.
It lives in the Americas.

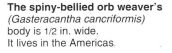

The water hyacinth's
(*Eichhornia crassipes*)
leaves are 6 in. long, and its
flower spike is 7 in. long.
It lives all over the world.

**The young red-sided
garter snake**
(*Thamnophis sirtalis parietalis*)
is 6 in. long.
It lives in North America.

The snapping turtle's
(*Chelydra serpentina*)
shell is 3 in. long.
It lives in the Americas.

The water lettuce's
(*Pistia stratiotes*)
leaves are 1 in. wide.
It lives all over
the world.

UNDERCOVER CRABS

AS THE TIDE GOES OUT, a shoreline of tangled roots and sticky mud is uncovered. Suddenly, dozens of fiddler crabs like these pop out of their burrows and scuttle around in search of food. They are scavengers, feeding on small particles of food, such as algae (simple plants), on the surface of the mud. When danger threatens, they dash back into their burrows for safety. Some fiddler crabs live in the stagnant (still) mud of the swamp, and some live in sand banks. Each crab has its own area, called a territory. The territories are very small, because there are so many other fiddler crabs sharing the swamp. Male fiddler crabs have one small pincer and one enormous one. They use the giant pincer to signal to females, and to scare away other males from their territory.

GUESS WHAT?
The male fiddler crab's huge pincer is very good for impressing other crabs, but its size can be a disadvantage. It is no use at all for gathering food, so the crab can only feed with its smaller pincer. Females can gather food with both their pincers.

A CLASH OF CLAWS
If two males confront each other, the smaller one is usually wise enough to retreat. Even two well-matched males settle most arguments simply by threatening each other with their claws. But if this fails, then a real fight breaks out. The crabs lock their large pincers together and wrestle until one of them gives in.

Inside each pincer there are strong muscles that open and shut it, so that the crab can hold on tightly to the claw of another male fiddler crab.

The crab's right claw is usually the larger one.

SPRINTING SIDEWAYS

Crabs have four pairs of long legs arranged along a wide, but short body. They can walk forward slowly, but each leg can only take a short step without tripping over the leg in front. By stepping sideways, the legs can take much bigger strides. When crabs are startled, they can run sideways very fast indeed.

MUD PIE

These crabs are good at getting food out of the mud. They scrape up a ball of mud with their pincers, then pass it to their mouthparts. These roll the ball around while the crab sucks all the nutrients out of it. Afterward, it drops these mud balls near its burrow. The mud balls are called "pseudofaeces," which means "false droppings."

FLAG-WAVING

The male fiddler crab uses his large pincer much like a flag. He spends a lot of his time waving it proudly at females he hopes to attract. Each kind of fiddler crab waves its claw in a special pattern, so that it only appeals to females of the same kind. This helps to avoid confusion, and it is useful in the swamp, where many kinds of fiddler crabs live close together.

The crab's eyes have long stalks that allow it to peep out over the rim of its burrow and watch for danger.

The small pincer gathers food.

The legs are made up of rigid segments, with flexible joints so they can bend.

FEARSOME FACES

GREEN IGUANAS ENJOY sunbathing in the leafy mangrove branches around the swamp. Their bright color helps conceal them from predators. If they are alarmed, these sprightly lizards jump into the water below and swim to safety. Male iguanas protect their territory by scaring away other males with a fierce display. They stand up tall, flatten their bodies, and stick out their dewlaps (neck flaps). This usually puts off the intruder, and real fights do not often take place. After mating, each female digs a burrow in warm, damp sand, and lays 20 to 30 eggs there. When the young hatch, they sleep and feed together, relying on safety in numbers, until they are old enough to protect themselves.

GUESS WHAT?
Common iguanas have extremely good eyesight and can see in color. One male iguana may perform its threatening display to another male more than 300 feet away.

LEAPING LIZARD
With its long legs and clawed toes, th iguana is a fast mover. Its body streamlined for speed, and the long ta helps it balance as it jumps. It sprin very fast, can run up tree trunks, an leap from branch to branch. Iguanas ar mainly herbivorous (plant-eating), s they do not have to hunt for prey, bu they do need to escape from hungr enemies, such as bird

The iguana uses its tail to balance the weight of its body. This is called counterbalancing.

The powerful back legs are good for running and jumping.

Scaly skin protects the body from damage, and stops it from drying out.

e iguana bites
f pieces of fruit
d leaves with its
rd mouth, then
ews them up
th its teeth.

This single row
of pointed scales
is called the
dorsal crest.

These tough,
protective scales are
made of a protein
called keratin.

his membrane
hin skin) is the
uana's ear.

DAYTIME DAZZLER

These common, or green,
iguanas are active during the day.
Their skin color helps them hide
from their enemies among the
leaves. But during the breeding
season, male iguanas need to attract
females to mate with. They become
an even more brilliant green, and
the patterns on their bodies get
much brighter.

DROOPY JAWS

The loose skin that hangs behind the
iguana's chin is called a dewlap.
Males have larger dewlaps than
females. Their jawbones work much
like umbrellas, spreading the skin
out. This makes the head look much
larger and more fierce than it really
is, and helps frighten off enemies.

The long, well-spread
toes have sharp claws
for gripping branches
and twigs.

A FISH OUT OF WATER

THE MUDSKIPPER'S NAME fits it perfectly. It spends more time skipping across the mudflats than swimming in water. It will even climb up a mangrove tree in search of food. Mudskippers spend most of their time out of the water, but they need to keep their skin moist. When they get too dry, they roll in puddles and wipe their faces with a wet fin. These fish can move much faster on land than in water. They hunt energetically for small creatures, such as insects, to eat. The mudskipper is not sociable, and if another mudskipper gets too close, it warns off the intruder by raising the fin on its back. When danger threatens, the mudskipper dives into the water and hides in the mud among the tangled mangrove roots. During the rainy season, these fish dig burrows in the mud so the female can give birth to her live young in safety.

FANTASTIC FINS

The mudskipper's fins are adapted so that it can walk, jump, swim, and even climb. The front pair of fins, called pectoral fins, look like little arms. The fish uses them for moving around on land. The second pair, called pelvic fins, are shorter and joined together underneath the body to make a kind of sucker. This sucker helps the mudskipper cling on to mangrove roots when it climbs.

POP-UP PEEPER

The mudskipper's bulging ey are close together on the top its head. They stick up so th the fish can see all around itse When the mudskipper swims, eyes peep out of the water. Th can move up and down like t periscopes of a submarine, ar allow the mudskipper to se above and below the wat at the same tim

These two fish may look as if they are being friendly, but in fact their dorsal fins are raised in anger.

Mudskippers can breathe through their skin as well as their gills.

When it is out of water, the mudskipper keeps its eyes moist by rolling them back into their sockets every so often.

These mottled colors blend in well with the patches of light and shade on the shores of tropical swamps.

The torpe shaped bo allows t mudskipper swim eas through wate

OXYGEN TANKS

Like all fish, the mudskipper breathes with its feathery gills. It waves water over them with its gill covers, and absorbs oxygen from the water into its blood. Before climbing out of the swamp, the mudskipper fills its large gill chambers with water. These act like oxgyen tanks, keeping the fish's blood supplied with oxygen while it is on land.

The gill covers shut tight when the mudskipper is on land to store water inside the gill chambers.

The upper part of the pectoral fin is strong and muscular to support the fish's weight.

This strangely shaped mouth is good for snapping up insects, spiders, and even small crabs.

This groove along the side of the fish is called the lateral line. It helps the fish keep its balance in the water.

Sharp teeth easily grab prey.

Suckerlike pelvic fins help the fish cling to slippery mangrove roots and rocks.

These stiff rays dig into the sand when the fish walks.

GUESS WHAT?
By curling its body to one side and suddenly straightening it, a mudskipper can flip itself as far as two feet in one movement.

MAKE IT SNAPPY

SNAPPING TURTLES LIVE in the still, warm waters of swamps and creeks. They are slow-moving creatures, but they have a hard shell and a ferocious bite for defending themselves. These quiet reptiles spend most of their time in shallow water, hiding among plants at the bottom of the swamp. If a fish or other prey swims by, a snapping turtle can shoot out its long neck and snap it up. Like most turtles and tortoises, snapping turtles have a varied diet. They feed on water plants and carrion (dead animals), as well as live prey. In summer, the females clamber onto land to lay their eggs, sometimes traveling overland to a good site. They lay between 20 and 30 round, white eggs in a hole that they dig with their back legs. The young hatch out of the eggs in autumn.

The nostrils are at the tip of the snout, so the turtle just has to poke its head out of the water to breathe in air.

A WALK IN THE WATER
This turtle's feet are adapted for moving under water and on land. The toes are webbed, which helps the turtle push water aside. But in spite of this, the snapping turtle is not very good at swimming. It usually gets around under water by walking along the bottom, using its claws to grip onto mud or rock.

A layer of algae hides the smooth scutes of the turtle's shell.

UNDER COVER
The smooth scutes covering the turtle's back are patterned with brown, olive, and yellow. But these colors are often hidden by a thick layer of algae (simple plants) that grows on the shell. When the turtle rests among the vegetation at the bottom of the swamp, this covering makes it almost invisible.

The turtle's legs are strong, but the weight of its body and shell slow it down, both on land and in water.

The long claws are good for walking on clay and sand.

The snapping turtle's tail is usually about the same length as its body.

The turtle uses its webbed feet for swimming.

TOOTHLESS TERROR

A snapping turtle does not have teeth. But it has very powerful jaws, and its mouth has a hard, sharp edge. These turtles can seriously wound larger animals. They may even bite off a finger or toe if you get too close. The cutting edge and the beaklike hook go on growing in the same way as our fingernails, so although biting wears them down, they never wear out.

GUESS WHAT?

When a snapping turtle's eggs are kept at a temperature of between 72°F and 82°F, male young will develop. Any other temperature produces females.

LIVING IN A BOX

The turtle's shell is made up of bones, joined together to make a protective box for the body. The skin covering the shell forms a tough layer of hard, thick scales, called scutes. Some kinds of turtles can pull their legs and head inside their hard shell for safety. But a snapping turtle's shell is much too small for it to do this, so it relies mostly on its nasty bite to scare off enemies.

The neck is surprisingly long when the turtle stretches it out.

The turtle's thick skin protects it from damage.

The bony shell is covered with tough, scaly skin for extra protection.

HANDSOME HUNTER

THE MANGROVE snake spends most of the day resting in the trees. The striking coloring looks as though it would be difficult to hide. But when it is quietly coiled up in the dappled shade of leafy branches, a mangrove snake is very hard to see. These snakes get their name because they usually live in mangrove swamps, but they are also found near fresh water. At night, they go out to hunt for prey, such as lizards and birds. Most poisonous snakes inject their venom by stabbing their long, curved fangs into their prey. The mangrove snake's fangs are near the back of its mouth, so it has to bite its prey in order to poison it. These snakes will eat almost any animal small enough to get in their mouths.

A transparent scale, called a brille, protects the snake's eyes.

WHOLE FOOD
Snakes can swallow animals bigger than their own head. They can do this because their jawbones are only loosely joined together by ligaments and muscles. Each side of the lower jaw can move to allow the food to go down the snake's throat.

SCARLET STRIPES

RED-SIDED GARTER SNAKES live near all kinds of fresh water, including lakes, streams, and swamps. They feed mainly on fish, frogs, and insects. In winter, garter snakes gather in large numbers in a sheltered place underground to hibernate. When warmer weather returns in spring, the snakes come out and bask in the sun. They slough (shed) their skin, and then mate. About three months later, the females give birth to around 20 live young, although large snakes may produce as many as 70 young.

Even when the snake's mouth is shut, its forked tongue flicks in and out through this notch in the upper jaw.

GUESS WHAT?
Snakes can swim, climb trees, and glide over rocks and along the ground. Instead of legs, they have long, powerful muscles that move the body, and large scales along the underside for a good grip.

GOING DOWN
Snakes have muscles that push food toward the stomach. Their ribs can move outward so food does not get stuck along the way. Between the scales, a snake's skin is very stretchy. The skin expands when a large meal is swallowed, but returns to its normal shape as soon as the meal has been digested.

Snakes have very flexible bodies because their backbones are made up of hundreds of tiny bony segments, called vertebrae.

The round pupil shows that these snakes are diurnal (active during the day). Nocturnal snakes (those active at night) have slit-shaped pupils, like the mangrove snake.

Between the scales, the stretchy skin can expand like a balloon if the snake eats a large meal.

20

FLOATING LOGS

FLOATING IN THE STILL water of tropical swamps or lakes, these caimans often look like harmless logs. They are related to alligators, and like them, their eyes and nostrils are set high up on the head. This means that even when the rest of the caiman's body is under water, it can see and breathe in air. Although this young caiman is small, it is a fierce predator, feeding mainly on insects and frogs. Adults prey on larger animals, including fish and mammals. In the breeding season, female caimans gather bits of plants with their mouths, then build huge mounds for their eggs. Each female lays up to 40 eggs in the middle of her mound. The rotting vegetation helps keep the eggs warm. After about three months, tiny caimans hatch out. They stay together in groups, watched over by one of the females, until they are strong enough to protect themselves from enemies, such as large snakes.

NO ESCAPE

When a caiman opens its mouth, you can see daggerlike teeth on both jaws. These jaws can snap shut on their prey with great force. The front teeth interlock, so there is little chance of escape for the unfortunate victim. Caimans cannot chew. If their prey is too big to swallow whole, they have to tear off bite-sized chunks.

Strong, sharp teeth crunch through shells.

The caiman's slit-shaped pupils help it hunt at night. The pupils expand in the dark, to make the best use of whatever light there is.

The caiman's snout turns up at the end, keeping the nostrils out of the water.

This dull, blotchy coloring helps young caiman hide from hungry predators until it is large enough to defend itself.

A flattened, muscular tail like this is ideal for swimming.

The front feet are good for digging. In dry weather, caimans often burrow into the mud, to shelter from the sun.

A caiman's legs are attached to the sides of its body. Caimans can run quite fast, but only over short distances.

BLACK WITH COLD

When caimans get too cold, they change their color. There are cells in the skin that contain a black pigment, called melanin. These cells expand when the temperature drops, and the skin turns black. Dark colors absorb heat well, so a black skin helps the caiman keep warm.

ony ridge looks
like a pair of
s, so this
n is called a
cled caiman.

Caimans have very good
hearing, both in and out of
water. Their ears are covered
with a thin membrane to keep
water from getting inside.

Unlike most
reptiles, a caiman
does not shed its skin in
one piece in order to grow.
Instead, it sheds each
scale separately,
replacing it with a
larger one.

This young caiman is
only 18 in. long. But it
may grow to be up to
8 ft. from head to tail.

GUESS WHAT?

When a caiman dives, it
can close its nostrils. It
also has a flap of skin to
close off its windpipe and
throat. This means that
the caiman can grab
prey in its mouth while it
is swimming. If it could
not close its nose and
throat, it might fill its
stomach and lungs with
water, and risk drowning.

SKIN AND BONES

Like all reptiles, caimans are covered in
scales. Their scales are tough, to protect
the body from damage. They also prevent
the caiman from drying out when it is
basking in the sun. Along the back and
belly the protective layer is even tougher,
because underneath the outer scales there
are plates of bone. These are called
osteoderms, which means "skin-bones."

PLANT PARADISE

THE WARM, WET environment of tropical swamps is perfect for plant life. Many different kinds of plants flourish here, including mosses, ferns, and trees. Some are completely aquatic, which means that they live submerged in the water. Water lettuces and water hyacinths float on the surface with their roots in the water. These plants can be carried along by water currents and breezes. The waterproof leaves have air-filled floats to keep them the right side up. Other plants, such as mangrove trees, grow in the shallow water at the edge of swamps. Their roots are firmly embedded in wet sand or mud. All swamp animals, including birds, insects, fish, and mammals, depend on the plants for food, and also for the oxygen that they produce. If there were no plants, the animals would all disappear, too.

SALT SOLUTION

Mangroves are the only trees that grow in salt water. Each kind has special roots that are adapted to help it breathe. These red mangroves have prop roots, which are partly exposed to the air. Oxygen enters through tiny holes, called lenticels, in the bark of the roots. Too much salt is poisonous to plants, and makes it difficult for them to take up water. The mangrove's leaves are waterproof, which keeps water from escaping.

SWAMP SALAD

When the water lettuce plant has space around it, it is a neat rosette of leaves floating on the water. New rosettes sprout at the tips of short stems, called stolons, that grow out at the sides. These eventually break off to form new plants. Water lettuces can quickly cover the surface. As they become more crowded, the leaves have less room to spread out, so they grow straight up.

There are silky hairs covering the leaves. Water rolls off them, so they do not become waterlogged and sink below the surface.

A spongy, air-fille swelling at the base each leaf stalk keep the plant afloa

This water lettuce plant has plenty of room to spread its leaves out over the water's surface.

These trailing, feathery roots absorb nutrients from the water.

GUESS WHAT?
Sometimes drifting twigs and leaves become entangled in clumps of water lettuce plants. This can make a floating island, which is strong enough to support the weight of birds, frogs, and sometimes even a Sumatran rhinoceros.

POLLUTION PATROL
The roots of water hyacinths and water lettuces are very good at absorbing important nutrients from the water. They also trap substances that pollute the water. Scientists have begun to use these floating plants to filter (strain) the water in polluted rivers and lakes.

The scent of water hyacinth flowers attracts insects, such as butterflies, that pollinate the plant.

Mangrove leaves are waterproof, to prevent too much water from evaporating into the air.

Like mangrove leaves, water hyacinth leaves have a waxy cuticle (skin) so they do not become waterlogged.

ARTFUL ARCHER

ARCHERFISH LIVE IN the warm, shallow waters of tropical mangrove swamps. They usually feed on insects, which they find on the surface of the water or flying close to it. But among the overhanging mangrove branches, there are many more tempting insects. The archerfish has a clever way of bringing one of these into range. It spits out a powerful jet of water that knocks the insect down so that the fish can snap it up! Female archerfish give birth to live young. The young swim together in groups, called schools. They are safer in large numbers because predators cannot decide which fish to attack. As archerfish grow larger, they leave the school to begin their adult lives by themselves.

WATER PISTOL

By pressing its tongue against a groove running along the roof of its mouth, the archerfish makes this part of its mouth into a narrow tube. When the fish spots an insect on a leaf overhead, it snaps its gill covers shut. This is like squeezing the trigger on a water pistol. It forces a jet of water out of the fish's mouth and through the air to hit the target.

The mouth opens upward so the fish can skim food from the surface of the water.

The scales are covered with a thin layer of skin and mucus (slime), which helps prevent infections.

The tail fin helps the fish swim forward fast, and acts like a boat's rudder to help it change direction.

Fish move their fins to change speed and direction.

LOUDED VISION

ght does not travel through water as
ell as it does through air. Swamp
ater is often cloudy, which makes it
ven harder to see through. But a
sh's eyes are adapted to make the
est of these difficult conditions, and
ey see most clearly in dim light. The
rcherfish has much better eyesight
an most fish. It needs it, because it
as to look through both water and
r when it takes aim at an insect.

The leaves and
flowers of mangrove
trees hang over the
water, providing
shade for fish and
other animals below.

The jet of water
must travel fast
enough to knock the
insect off the leaf.

Many kinds of
insects, like this fly,
are attracted to the
warm, shady
environment of the
mangrove swamp.

GUESS WHAT?
Young archerfish often
miss their target. With
practice, they improve
their aim, and learn to
use the tip of their tongue
to direct the jet of water.
An adult can score a
direct hit on an insect
up to 5 feet above the
surface of the water.

Fish do not have
eyelids. Instead, a
clear layer of skin
protects their eyes
from damage.

When the fish spits,
its mouth opens just
enough to allow the
water through.

From above, these
black patches look
like shadows made
by leaves. They
make it difficult
for enemies to
see the fish.

SIDELINES
Along each side of the
archerfish's body is an invisible
line called the lateral line. This is
a narrow tube that contains tiny,
highly sensitive organs. These
organs detect vibrations (tiny
movements) traveling through
the water, so the fish can tell
when food, danger, or others of
its own kind are nearby.

VANISHING TRICK

WITH A FLASH OF COLOR, the timid purple gallinule disappears into the reeds to hide. You may not often see this bird, but you will certainly hear it. Its cackling song rings out clearly over the waters of the swamp. Families of birds use quiet, clicking calls to stay in contact with one another. Gallinules spend much time paddling in the mud, looking for food. In the breeding season, each male and female pair uses bits of plants to build an untidy nest, usually hidden in the reed beds. The female lays up to six eggs in the nest, where they will be warm and dry. The chicks hatch out about four weeks later. Their legs grow quickly, so they are soon able to follow their parents on short trips. At six to eight weeks old, the young birds are ready to leave the nest.

This bright red part of the bill is called the frontal shield.

The powerful bill can bite into hard seeds and roots.

PLAYING IT SAFE
Purple gallinules are rather shy birds. They stay close to the edge of the swamp, and rarely fly over open expanses of water where they would be exposed to danger. When possible, purple gallinules prefer to hide or dive to escape from enemies.

GUESS WHAT?
Purple gallinules often build platforms high up among the reeds, where they can sunbathe in the early morning.

The feathers are coated with oil. This prevents them from getting waterlogged when the bird swims or dives.

GING FOR FOOD

inules often dig for food in the
l. They eat seeds, plant stems,
cts, other birds' eggs, and even
d fish. If a meal is too large to
llow, the bird holds it with its
, toes and breaks up the
l with its bill.

FOLLOW THE TAIL

The short, stumpy tail of an
adult purple gallinule is
blue on top, but bright
white underneath. This
makes it easy for a young
chick to follow its parents
on both land and water
when it first ventures
out of the nest.

*These long, stiff
feathers are important
for flying. They are
called primary feathers.*

*These short tail
feathers do not trail in
the mud or get caught
in vegetation.*

HIGH STEPPING

This bird does not have webbed
feet, like those of many water birds.
But it still swims and dives, and its
long toes are useful for grasping
and climbing. The bird picks its way
through tangled plants and reeds,
closing its toes to avoid catching
them. Then, as it puts each foot
down, it spreads the toes out again,
so it does not sink into the mud.

*This bird's long,
splayed toes spread its
weight out over a large
area. This means it can
stand and walk on
floating leaves.*

*A purple gallinule
can wade through
soft mud on its long
legs without getting
its feathers soiled
and sticky.*

*The gallinule
pulls its toes
together when it
picks up its feet.*

SPIKY SPIDERS

THESE STRANGELY SHAPED spiders look almost unreal as they scuttle around on their huge, fragile webs. Spiny-bellied orb weavers, such as these, make their homes among the leaves and flowers of mangrove trees. The spiky shape and the bright, shiny patterns on their bodies make them easy to spot. But the spikes also make the spiders difficult to eat, and this puts off birds, lizards, and other predators looking for a meal. These female spiders are fat with eggs. When they lay their eggs, they wrap them in a bright green cocoon made of silk. They attach the cocoon to the underside of a mangrove leaf, where it is well hidden. The young hatch inside the cocoon, molt (shed) their skin once, and bite their way through to the outside world.

GUESS WHAT?
Male spiny-bellied orb weavers are tiny. Around 15 males could fit on the back of just one of these female spiders.

These cone-shaped spikes are made of a hard protein called chitin.

The spider's abdomen is smooth and shiny. Water runs off it quickly, so it does not become waterlogged.

Some of these tiny hairs on the spider's legs are very sensitive to touch. Others can detect the air currents made by flying insects.

Each thread is thin and stretchy, but it is also very strong.

This tough cuticle (outer skin) protects the spider's body.

FOOD STORAGE
Spiders are fierce predators, with mouthparts adapted to dealing quickly with struggling prey. Some of the insects that blunder into a web have stingers, or other weapons, which they could use to attack the spider if they had the chance. So the spiky spider bites her prey with her sharp fangs. These inject a venom that paralyzes the insect without killing it, so the flesh stays fresh until the spider needs to eat it.

Three minute claws on each foot help the spider grip its web and move quickly toward a trapped insect.

The petals of mangrove flowers are covered in waterproof wax. This prevents too much water escaping from the plant.

Hidden underneath the spikes are the spinnerets, which the spider uses to spin its web.

STICK AROUND

These spiders spin large, round webs, called orb webs, on mangrove branches. They walk along strong threads that spread out from the center, like the spokes of a bicycle wheel. Sticky threads arranged in a spiral shape on the web trap insects.

SPIN IT OUT

Spiders make liquid silk in special glands in their abdomens, then squeeze it out through their spinnerets. These are right at the tip of the abdomen, and work much like tiny tubular fingers. They pull the silk until it is the right thickness, and attach each thread firmly to the web.

INDEX

GLOSSARY

Abdomen the rear part of the body
Algae simple plants, such as seaweeds
Aquatic living in water
Brille a transparent scale that protects a snake's eye
Chitin the strong substance that makes up an animal's exoskeleton
Cuticle the outer layer of an animal or plant
Dewlap a fold of loose skin that hangs below the throat of some animals, such as iguanas
Diurnal active during the day
Gills organs that animals, such as fish, use to take in oxygen from the water
Herbivorous plant-eating
Hibernate to rest or sleep during the cold months of the year
Keratin the substance that makes up hair, fur, and nails
Lateral line the line of sensitive cells along each side of a fish's body
Melanin a black or brown pigment found in an animal's hair, skin, or eyes
Membrane a thin, elastic skin

Mucus a slimy, often poisonous substance that certain animals produce
Nares nostrils
Nocturnal active at night
Nutrients substances, such as minerals, which plants and animals need in order to stay healthy
Ocelli the simple eyes of an insect or other animal
Osteoderm a bony plate in the skin that gives an animal extra protection
Oxygen a gas that plants give out, and which animals need for breathing
Photosynthesis the use of sunlight by plants to produce the energy for growing
Pollination the transfer of pollen from the male part of a flower to the female part, where fertilization takes place
Setae special hairs on the body
Sloughing molting (snakes and lizards)
Spinnerets tiny silkhandling organs in spiders and some insects
Venom poison
Vertebrae the bony segments that make up an animal's backbone